# Gowri's Contemplation

# Acknowledgement

I believe that if you dream to do something and you work hard ,you can achieve it.This book is my dream come true and I owe this book to my parents because when I started scribbling small poems ,my mother encouraged me to write further and helped me in assembling my poems. My father is a strong influence for me and he encouraged me to never give up whatever happens in life. They both make me strong.

I am very thankful to my teachers who guided me to explore the world through books.They never discouraged me. I thank my little brother for giving me moral support and ideas. Last but not the least I thank almighty for blessings me with a supportive environment and beautiful thoughts where I can nurture my talent.

# Magic spaceship

Our homework was
incomplete
Because they weren't on
due
Suddenly something
appeared on the window
It was yellow,green and
blue
It came in the classroom
And swooped me up in
time
Then an angry voice
reported
"Come on wake up Gowri"

# Food

I love food
Because they are tasty
Some in don't like
Cause they are really nasty
In all ailment
Food comes in need
But who that cannot eat
them
Are really sick indeed

# Sand dunes

I am in a desert
Standing on some sand
I am very thirsty
With nothing in my hand
I start to cry
Then I start to think
I CAN SEE WATER!
Then I blink and blink
Hushh... I wake up
Then I see the date
I gasp in amazement
actually I'm late!

# The fish pot

Blue and green
In the sky
Like the sea
In my eye
May be happy
May be sad
May be joyful
May be bad
The gift is coming
In a big bowl
A baby fish
Will it smell foul

## Diwali time

An Indian house At Diwali night
Will be brighter than the Sunlight
Diwali time Has the fun for you
Diwali is a  festival For foodies too
Bright dresses,sweets, lights,
Family and friends to see
Joyful mood that shine so bright
No need to wait... FOR DIWALI
delight!!

# Maths test

I come in class
Trembling in fear
“Come on little Mia
Start the exam now dear”
All of the questions
Running in my mind
I try to catch them
But no answers I could find
I am down
I give the test
Mrs leela says
“Do your very, very best!”
Today is the day
I get the test
“OMG” I cried
Cause I was better than my past

# The Mythical Forest

Once I had a picnic
Next to a forest
Suddenly my dog barked
As if there was a huge feast

I had no idea
But he started to run
I just started following him
Maybe this is for fun

I saw a twilight
Over a tree
I walked over
Just to see

It was the sunlight
Shining off a small plain
I didn't know that
Nature had so much in greens.

# Music

When i hear music
so far or so rare
it will bring happiness
or either despair

It may be modern
or it may be old
whatever age it is
it will always be gold

# The lonely wind

Night & morning
Moon and sun
Waiting and watching
Is no more fun

But just thinking of it
The lonely wind's mind
It will be sitting there
With no one to find

And the rain
Look at it too
But wait a minute
Hailstones coming soon

continued...

**Will they meet up again**

**No one else Is there in the dark Only the wind Will he make a mark? Just then in time Wind's friend just came He was called lightning**

# My birthday

Tomorrow is the day
It will be very good
Tomorrow is my birthday
I will get lots of food

A pink fluffy fluff
On a brown chocolate ca
Why am I thinking this?
When is it going to bake?

I am really excited
I could burst into a hundred stars
I just have to be patient
I'll get a million chocolate bars

## Continued.....

Why is it taking time?
I really just can't wait
Wait! Or am I just thinking
OR AM I JUST LATE?!

Why can't I sleep
I'm just excited
My birthday is tomorrow
It okay I'm fine

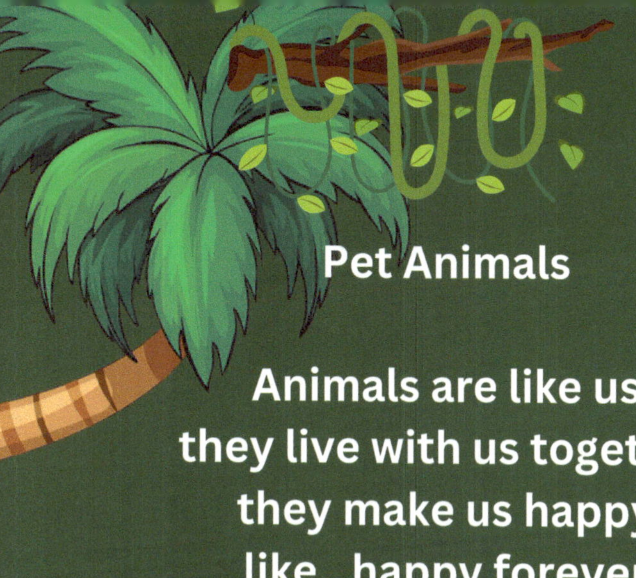

# Pet Animals

Animals are like us
they live with us together
they make us happy
like.. happy forever

Each of them
are of different types
domestic and wild
untamed and tamed

We all always play
with cats, dogs, fishes and parrots
but all these animals
are better than humans
because............
they are thankful to their masters

# The Earth

Once a drop of water
Gets wasted from a tap
People will start to cry
because others need water asap

Once you get water
You need to use it properly
Once another life is helpless
You need to help them happily

When u use the three r's
The world starts going on
If others copy you
The earth stays long

Soo many things destroy the earth
Most of this is true
If u help us save the Earth
You are a savior too

# Toys

Toys are for kids and
they come in different sizes
It doesn't matter..
If  they are winning gifts or
prizes!

Some kids take their toys
in their room, their bed and
outside
sometimes rarely they play
with them and keep aside

everyone likes them
whether big or small
they are colourful
they're something for all

**Family- a school**

A family consists of
many members
with love,care and compassion
you can never expect from others

You stay together
in ups and downs
You never have to be formal
from dusk to dawn

Maybe we have siblings
They can be young or old
Even they can be a girl or a boy
But you should treat them as gold

We learn lessons of life
trust.kindness and gratitude
unknowingly from our family
to reach high altitude

# Ice cream

Chocolate or vanilla
pink,cream or white
I love Ice creams
to relish day and night

Everyone likes icecreams
for no reason or clue
My friends love it so much
like paper and glue

There are many flavours
unimaginable delight
stick, cone or wafer cups
I hold it very tight

oh its so wonderful to think of
Ice creams yummy
but
“dont eat Ice creams during winters”
says my mummy

## Gowri's day out

I look at my teacher
Ah' she is so kind
I think of my future
Now I think of the time

Suddenly teacher calls me
And I say "oh my"
I was day dreaming
and now I am shy

She said "were you listening?"
I look at my friends
they all were giggling
and i nodded at once

I walk to the board
And write "102"
In my mind everyone said
"WE LOVE YOU"

www.ingramcontent.com/pod-product-compliance
Lightning Source LLC
LaVergne TN
LVHW021327160826
845679LV00002B/509

*9798897246793*